THE LOVE LIVES OF BIRDS

THE LOVE LIVES OF
Birds

Courting and Mating Rituals

LAURA ERICKSON

Storey Publishing

The mission of Storey Publishing is to serve our customers by publishing practical information that encourages personal independence in harmony with the environment.

Edited by Deborah Burns
Art direction and book design by Alethea Morrison
Text production by Slavica A. Walzl
Indexed by Samantha Miller
Illustrations by © Veronica B. Lilja/peppercookies.com
Additional watercolor backgrounds by © Katie Eberts

Storey books are available at special discounts when purchased in bulk for premiums and sales promotions as well as for fund-raising or educational use. Special editions or book excerpts can also be created to specification. For details, please call 800-827-8673, or send an email to sales@storey.com.

Storey Publishing
210 MASS MoCA Way
North Adams, MA 01247
storey.com

Printed in China by R.R. Donnelley
10 9 8 7 6 5 4 3 2 1

Library of Congress Cataloging-in-Publication Data on file

For my own lifelong mate, Russell,
who gave me my first cloudless days, balmy nights, books, babies,
and birds, and has stuck with me for decades longer
than the oldest swan on record.

Contents

Looking for Mr. or Ms. Right

HOW DO BIRDS FIND A MATE? The approaches of different species are as varied as those of humans. Some birds seem like Casanovas or even Marquises de Sade, while others seem as courtly and reticent as the most genteel Jane Austen characters. Cranes and swans have the leisure we humans do to spend months or even years making a permanent selection, even as Arctic shorebirds must make their choice within days, or even hours, of arriving on their breeding grounds so they can raise young before heading south again.

As with humans, bird species use different combinations of factors to judge members of the opposite sex. The quality and persistence of a male's song, the energy and style of his courtship displays, how well a female responds to his overtures, how well the two coordinate dance moves or song duets, the quality and quantity of romantic food offerings, the intensity and color of plumage or body parts — each species uses some combination of these cues, and more, to identify the ideal mate.

Age is an important criterion for birds: most want the oldest, most experienced mate they can find. Birds don't carry a passport or birth certificate, so how can they reveal their age to a prospective mate? Mockingbirds learn new songs throughout life, so the more songs in a male's repertoire, the older on average he is. Both male and female hawks of some species start out with yellow eyes, which over months and years turn orange and then ruby red. Young Cedar Waxwings have no red tips on their flight feathers; these tiny markings appear and then increase in number as the birds grow older. Year-old male American Redstarts resemble grayish and yellow females; they are fully capable of breeding, but females prefer mates bearing the black and orange plumage of older males, only settling for a younger one when no older males are available.

For most wild birds, it's impossible to be too old to make an ideal mate, because for both sexes, the time between a mature bird losing its competitive edge and dying is usually very short, long before the bird is no longer physiologically fertile. One female Laysan Albatross still reared a chick when she was at least 67 years old! In only a few species do birds seem to have a "sweet spot" between being too young and too old. The blue foot color on boobies tends to grow duller with age, yet many of these older males still succeed in attracting mates.

Beyond these very basic criteria, scientists don't understand what leads two birds to select each other. Is it a simple matter of proximity and chance? Do birds flirt? Might some want sparks to fly in a kind of magic before they'll commit? We may use "the birds and the bees" as a metaphor for courtship and sex, but our understanding of the fundamentals of just how birds establish and sustain relationships is superficial and rudimentary.

That's okay. As Walt Whitman wrote, "You must not know too much, or be too precise or scientific about birds ... a certain free margin, and even vagueness — perhaps ignorance, credulity — helps your enjoyment of these things."

ADÉLIE PENGUIN

Rocks Are a Hen's Best Friend

*I*n many species, males offer prospective mates food or nesting materials, and expect sex when a female accepts a gift, but this is virtually always in the context of forming and strengthening a pair bond. The female learns what kind of provider the male is, and food helps her body get into top shape for producing eggs.

The exchange of payment or gifts for sex without the context of building a lasting connection wouldn't seem to make sense for birds, so engaging in sexual activity for payment wouldn't seem at all likely in the natural world.

The exchange of payment or gifts for sex without the context of building a lasting connection wouldn't seem to make sense for birds.

Or would it? The Adélie Penguin, a small Antarctic bird, pairs off and starts nesting in late winter, when ice and snow cover the ground. To keep the eggs a bit warmer, and also to protect them from being inundated with meltwater, Adélies lay their eggs on a platform of stones. But as spring progresses, meltwater becomes deeper, requiring even more stones after all the easiest-to-find ones have been taken.

Desperate times call for desperate measures, and some female Adélies offer to have sex with one or more single males in exchange for stones to build up their own nests. Sometimes a female manages to initiate mutual courtship behaviors with an unpaired male, grab a stone, and leave without actually mating with him. And after one brief sexual encounter, a female took 62 stones from the unwitting single male over a period of an hour. Nesting males, equally desperate for stones, don't object to the means by which their mates gather them, and thus their otherwise monogamous relationships don't end up on the rocks.

A pair of Adélies spend six weeks or more building up their rock collection and courting before settling into egg production and parental responsibilities. To attract his mate in the first place and then hold her interest, the male displays, stretching his head and neck up and pointing his bill vertically; then he flaps his outstretched wings while making a very loud call.

The extended honeymoon probably helps cement the pair bond, important in a species that will from then on carry on a long-distance relationship.

The parent incubating the eggs must stay on the nest as the other heads out to sea to feed. Adélies nest close enough to the water that the feeding parent is gone for just a day or two before returning to take its turn, but the two don't spend much time together during the switch.

Some Adélie Penguin mates almost certainly find each other the following year, but their lives are so fraught with danger and their nesting colonies so crowded that they don't expect to find the same mate year after year and can't afford to spend much time looking. They take life, rocks, and love, as they come.

IN HARM'S WAY

The Adélie Penguin breeds on ice-free land, but it depends on sea ice the rest of the year and is being badly affected by climate change. The reduction in sea ice has caused populations of Adélies in the Antarctic Peninsula to plummet by 65 percent during the past 25 years.

AMERICAN CROW

Tender Romantics

O f all birds, those in the crow family are perhaps the most humanlike in their intelligence, devotion to family, and even their xenophobia regarding strangers. But some humans use them to symbolize malevolence, such as Edgar Allan Poe's Raven, the crows in Alfred Hitchcock's *The Birds*, and the pets of many Disney witches.

If we pay attention to the interactions between courting and mated crows, we can't miss their tender, loyal attachment to each other. Pairs of crows keep their public displays of affection quiet and subtle, filled with the kind of affectionate yet dignified intimacy that call to mind the witty, elegant married couple from the *Thin Man* movies of the 1930s and '40s. Yes, crows are the Nick and Nora Charles of the bird world.

Crows could never bring themselves to perform a gauche dance or over-the-top love song. Each pair is mostly inseparable but limit themselves to quiet billing, mostly when no one, avian or human, seems to be looking. They also engage in *allopreening*, gently running their bill through the other's feathers as Nora might smooth the lapel on Nick's suit or fix his tie. Their repartee is quiet and subtle, too.

Until they're ready to breed, young crows spend each nesting season helping their parents or other nearby pairs by serving as sentinels, finding nesting materials and food for the female and nestlings, and helping with nest sanitation.

That nesting period also happens to be the only time of year when settled couples are interested in sex. Unattached birds apparently feel their oats, too, and some get a crush on a nesting bird. Young males often approach in hopes of a romantic interlude, but pairs stick too close together to allow much hanky-panky.

Like Nick and Nora Charles, crows may not flaunt their love, but it's solid. In one study following more than 100 tagged pairs of crows in California and Oklahoma over the course of several years, some pairs remained together for at least 9 years, and only one pair "divorced" during the entire course of the study.

Forming such a sturdy pair bond takes time. Crows delay breeding until females are at least 2 and males at least 3 years old; most wait even longer.

WHAT HE DID FOR LOVE

Kevin McGowan of the Cornell Lab of Ornithology tells a story that could have come from a classic film noir about a female crow who did have extra-pair sex with a younger male; then the younger male killed her older mate. Subsequently she double-crossed the younger male and mated with a different male, forcing the younger one back home to his parents. Fortunately, most crows stick to the faithful Nick and Nora script.

This gives them plenty of time to observe experienced adults and to develop their own wooing techniques. They join feeding and roosting flocks, giving them lots of opportunities to mingle with their own and the opposite sex, allowing them to form attachments of various kinds with other young birds before forming a permanent pair bond with their one and only.

Slowly but surely, each Nick and Nora will find each other and keep the crow population thriving.

Crows engage in allopreening, gently running their bill through the other's feathers as Nora might smooth the lapel on Nick's suit or fix his tie.

AMERICAN ROBIN

Old-Fashioned Love Songs

For many northerners, the robin's song is the most welcome sign of spring. Some robins overwinter in Canadian provinces and the northernmost states, feeding on berries in sociable flocks. Wintering robins show no interest in sex or property ownership and virtually never sing. It's when males start arriving on their breeding territories, usually wherever the 24-hour temperatures are averaging 37°F (2.8°C), that they break into song, legitimately becoming the "first robins of spring."

Females don't winter as far north as males, and they seldom arrive on a breeding territory until local males have worked out their property lines. They are almost certainly attracted by the quality of both the male's song and his territory, but the biggest factor in mate selection for both sexes is breast feather coloration. They both want a mate whose color matches their own. The males might be singing "I Want a Girl (Just like the Girl That Married Dear Old Dad)," with the females responding in kind.

After a female arrives on a territory and pairs up with the male, she may need more time than he does to get into the mood for romance. Building her nest revs up her hormones, but to start, she needs mud, its availability depending on rainfall. As soon as construction starts in earnest, she is ready for romantic and domestic bliss.

Every morning the male starts singing well before dawn, while it's still quite dark. He makes time for breakfast when worms are first visible in the dim light, but he isn't thinking only of food. When his mate joins him, he struts around her, tail spread and elevated, wings fluttering, throat inflated. She finds it all irresistible. She may approach him, touching his open bill with her own, or she may cut to the chase. This early-morning rendezvous is often the only time the pair will mate that day.

STILL THE ONE?

If both robins of a pair survive the winter, the following spring they may or may not return to the area and may or may not return to each other. Whether a pair's love song could be "Still the One" or "Gonna Get Along Without You Now" seems random. So a wedding card depicting a pair of robins might not be quite appropriate if you're hoping the couple will still be together on their first anniversary.

She spends the rest of the day feeding, resting, and working on the nest. Her mate may bring her a few nest materials and sometimes seems to offer advice; whether she takes it is anybody's guess. Their early-morning trysts continue as she finishes the nest and lays a clutch of about four eggs.

Her mate may bring her a few materials and sometimes seems to offer advice; whether she takes it is anybody's guess.

She loses interest in sex when she starts incubating the full clutch, but as soon as the nestlings fledge, passion is reignited in both parents. They can produce three or even four batches of young in a single season. Then in late summer both of them lose interest in sex and territory as they prepare for fall migration and winter survival. Come spring, they'll feel a resurgence of romantic feelings, and he'll once again burst out singing those old-fashioned love songs.

AMERICAN WOODCOCK

Cyrano de Bergerac

*A*merican Woodcocks are also known as timberdoodles, bogsuckers, and hokumpokes. These shy birds spend their days hunkered down on the forest floor, slurping up earthworms with their improbably long proboscises. The bill's flexible tip and long length allow the bird to probe more than 2 inches into the slimy soil to pull up worms.

Ever watchful even as it searches for food beneath, the woodcock can spot predators sneaking up from any direction. It's hard to imagine this quiet, bashful loner ever finding the means to reproduce.

Something in the twilight of a spring evening causes a transformation.

But something in the twilight of a spring evening causes a transformation. As dusk deepens, the male finds a clearing, squats, and belches out an occasional buzzy *peent*. Then all at once he rises in an elegant sky dance, his wings singing with every beat, a delicate twittering that communicates love and longing as he spirals up toward the sky.

He's hard to pick out in the dark, but if we detect his silhouette passing by the moon, we can sometimes follow him through the spiral. When he reaches a height of 350 feet or so, almost seeming to touch low clouds, he bursts into poetry in the form of rich, melodic chirping, then falls like a spent leaf back to earth to resume his quiet existence once again. *Peent!*

Over the course of the evening, for many evenings during the spring, he'll transform himself over and over, this Cyrano de Bergerac of the bird world, short of beauty, long of beak, capable of composing irresistible expressions of love in the evening sky.

And irresistible he is. An avian Roxanne, as shy and introverted as Cyrano himself and with an even longer beak, gravitates to where he lands, eager to produce offspring that will share genes with this enthralling poet of the night sky. The two meet covertly, quietly, under cover of darkness. She may return several times for evening trysts as she lays her clutch of four eggs, but then she focuses on motherhood.

I COULD HAVE DANCED ALL NIGHT

How do male woodcocks learn to do their sky dance? Each breeding male defends his own dance territory, but other males, perhaps inexperienced one-year-olds, gather nearby. When the dancing male takes off on his flight, those other males often call *peent*, quieting when he returns to earth. They may be observing his moves in hopes of copying them one day in the future.

Her chicks hatch out within a few hours of one another, eyes already open. They stay snug and warm beneath their mother for a few hours as they dry out and then venture from the nest. She feeds them for at least a week, but the toddlers start probing the soil on their own within 3 or 4 days. They'll make their first awkward ascents after just 2 weeks, and within a few more days may make sustained flights.

In about 5 weeks, the chicks disperse; by the next spring, these little ones will be acting out their parents' spring rituals, too. And like their parents, the rest of the year they'll lead solitary lives. Woodcocks may quietly feed near one another in good wormy places but seldom interact.

Only in spring does the night sky temporarily release males from their inhibitions, and their expressions of love release females from theirs. The rest of the year, these shy Cyranos lead quiet lives, alone again, naturally.

American Woodcocks are also known as timberdoodles, bogsuckers, and hokumpokes.

ARCTIC TERN

Going the Distance

Arctic Terns may or may not have sunny dispositions, but they see more sunlight every year than any other species in the world. They breed from the Arctic Ocean down to coastal Maine and Cape Cod, and they spend the southern summer on the edges of the ice pack around Antarctica.

Terns are so aggressive that they sometimes kill each other in territorial battles. That level of aggression has to be switched off before they can safely approach a mate. Courtship routines ensure that two birds can trust each other to become steady, reliable partners.

Despite the birds' ferocity, raspy tern voices seem to be duetting about the eternal nature of their love. One pair of Common Terns maintained their pair bond year after year for at least 14 years; Arctic Terns almost certainly maintain such lasting bonds, too.

To find a permanent partner, an available male performs what birders call a "low flight" display over a nesting colony. Carrying a fish, he beats his wings rapidly, holding them higher above his body than in normal flight, and then locks them in a shallow V-position, making a loud "advertising call."

If he attracts a female's interest, she joins him in flight. He'll point his bill down, tilting his black cap away from her in an "aerial bent posture"; she'll fly over him with a straight posture, wings below horizontal, making a begging call. Then he zigzags toward his territory a few times. She'll follow him or move on.

If she alights with him, he offers her the fish he was carrying. Sometimes she spurns it; sometimes he reconsiders and eats it himself or flies off to offer it to another female; sometimes "she" is actually a male masquerading as a female to grab the prize for his own sweetheart. The first few times a female tries to accept the offering, the male may be slow to relinquish it, and both may tug at it for a bit.

Sometimes "she" is actually a male masquerading
as a female to grab the prize for his own sweetheart.

They take their relationship literally to the next level with their "high flight" display, initiated by either the male or female. The two rise higher and higher, sometimes more than 100 meters up, making various aerial maneuvers to strengthen their synchronicity and compatibility.

Making a nest scrape on the ground leads to mate-feeding, an important component of their honeymoon as the female's body prepares to ovulate. This sexually charged romantic dining continues until she lays the first egg. For the next few days, he continues to bring her fish and they still have plenty of sex, but now always at the nest, guarding the egg against gulls and other predators.

After the second egg is laid, the pair lose interest in sex as their focus switches to parenthood. They may or may not winter together, but come spring, when the male makes his "low flight" display, if she's there, they won't spend nearly as much time and energy testing each other. Their already-established trust hastens their second or third honeymoon. Banded Arctic Terns have lived together for more than 30 years, their partnerships outlasting many human marriages.

PACKING A WALLOP

The Arctic Tern's daintiness shouldn't be mistaken for fragility. On its nesting territory, this ferocious little bird may attack humans 800 times heavier than it, and one bloodied a polar bear 4,000 times its weight! To attack, they cruise in from above to make a quick, sharp jab with the beak, then dart away. People approaching a nesting colony must wear hard hats and heavy protection over their backs to avoid being wounded.

BALD EAGLE

This Old House

*F*or 40 years, the PBS program *This Old House* has documented the renovations of old houses. Each project can take 2 or 3 months to complete. A few birds renovate and reuse old nests, but parasites multiply quickly in summer, and nests are constructed of biodegradable materials that don't hold up over time, so most birds start from scratch for every new batch of babies.

Bald Eagles construct their nests to last generations. Each pair devotes more time each year on nest renovations than it would take to binge-watch an entire season of *This Old House*. Indeed, Bald Eagles seem as devoted to the nest as to one another. When an eagle is killed, its mate may quickly attract a new mate to that sturdily built nest, which may have a far longer life span than the birds who built it.

> *Bald Eagles seem as devoted to the nest as to one another.*

Whether an experienced pair must rebuild after their nest tree toppled or a young pair is building their starter home, the first task is to find an appropriate site. These easy fliers don't need to be too close to their favorite fishing areas. It's better to nest in a sturdy tree or on an inaccessible cliff with a long commute than a flimsier tree or ground site that a wolf or bobcat might discover.

In northern forests, a white pine is ideal. This long-lived "super canopy" species rises above the forest, making it easy for a bird with a 6- or 7-foot wingspan to glide into. The whorls of branches often have gaps, allowing the eagle to nest near but not at the very top, so the nest will be less conspicuous and branches above will protect nestlings from the elements.

To last a lifetime, eagles usually choose a living tree. They also take the neighborhood into consideration, preferring to nest near one or two tall dead trees useful for perching.

Both the male and female gather construction materials, lugging sticks from as far as a mile away, and both sexes interweave them into a basic nest bowl. They use grasses, mosses, cornstalks, Spanish moss, and other clumps

SECOND HOMES

Eagles have such an intense focus on nest construction that many pairs build a second nest, which they can use if their primary nest fails. Focusing together on shared building projects may help synchronize their behaviors and physiological states in the same way that their aerial courtship does, ensuring that their partnership is strong enough to endure the annual 4- or 5-month commitment of raising young together.

of materials to fill the spaces between the sticks and to line the nest cup, adding some of their own feathers.

Working together on this shared project seems an essential component of the eagles' pair bond. In fact, that working partnership stirs romantic urges. Eagles initiate their dramatic aerial courtship displays during the time they're fixing up the nest.

Eagles initiate their dramatic aerial courtship displays during the time they're fixing up the nest.

Throughout the period that they're raising young and especially after the young fledge, the pair continues to add nest materials. In areas where eagles remain year-round, pairs work on their nests throughout winter, with a big surge of remodeling activity as courting resumes.

Eagles apparently take "building a relationship" quite literally.

BELTED KINGFISHER

Group Hug!

*I*n the final episode of the '70s sitcom *The Mary Tyler Moore Show*, when the characters make their tearful farewell, they join in a group hug. When they need tissues from Mary's desk, they stay in that tight huddle as they shuffle over.

The Belted Kingfisher, a loner from the moment it leaves its parents until it dies, grants a brief annual exception for a mate and chicks. Yet it's the only bird who engages in group hugs and shuffles en masse from one spot to another, just like Mary's newsroom gang. How? And why?

Kingfishers have exceptionally short legs and small, oddly shaped feet, the outer toes fused along most of the length. They can neither walk nor hop — to move when they can't fly, they shuffle. The weird foot shape is ideal for excavating a burrow in a sand bank. Kingfishers use their oversized bill to break up the soil and their thickened feet to shovel the dirt out the entrance.

In spring when kingfishers arrive on their breeding grounds, males establish their nesting territory. Courtship is practical and low key. If a female alights on a perch in a male's territory and he's interested, he'll fly over with a fish. If she's interested, she'll shuffle toward him, and he'll shuffle toward her. When they're side by side, she takes the fish, and they mate.

After that, he'll sometimes bring another fish to her, or he'll perch with his catch and wait for her to come to him — either approach leads to sex. Sometimes when he spies her on a perch, he flies over and without his even offering a fish, they mate.

The male selects the spot in a bank where they'll take turns excavating the nest. One works while the other calls from a nearby perch, maybe cheering its mate on, maybe offering "helpful" suggestions. They work mostly in the morning, stopping if it rains. They may not resume work for a week or more if the ground is too wet after a rainy spell. In fine weather, it may take just 3 days to finish the burrow, which extends up to 36 feet into the bank, ending in an earthy chamber.

Chicks huddle together to stay warm and to ensure that no stragglers go unnoticed at feeding time.

YOU AND ME AGAINST THE WORLD

Male and female Belted Kingfishers are about the same size. The male establishes the pair's nesting territory, which they both defend against other kingfishers. In most bird species with this kind of territorial system, including many other species of kingfishers, the male is the more brightly colored sex. But female Belted Kingfishers are brighter, with a rusty red belly band and flanks.

The birds mate a few times each day as they excavate and then throughout egg laying, which may last another week or more. When the clutch of five to eight eggs is complete, they lose interest in sex, which doesn't change their relationship much because they hadn't seemed all that interested to begin with.

Both parents incubate, the female at night, and they virtually never leave the eggs unattended. After the chicks hatch, when a parent comes in to regurgitate a blob of partially digested fish, it feeds the chicks closest to it. They huddle together to stay warm and to ensure that no stragglers go unnoticed at feeding time. If one chick moves even a little in one direction, all the chicks in the huddle follow.

Every standoffish adult survived as a chick by this cuddling. Yet when it finally emerged from the nest cavity, shaking the dirt off its wings, it also shook off that friendly impulse for the rest of its life.

BLACK-CAPPED CHICKADEE

Living in Jane Austen's World

*I*t is a truth universally acknowledged, that a single bird in possession of a good territory, must be in want of a mate. With a bit of tweaking, Jane Austen's opening sentence in *Pride and Prejudice* describes many birds, but her depiction of English society in the eighteenth century most closely mirrors the life of the Black-capped Chickadee.

Chickadees lead lives more provincial than did Austen herself, staying within their neighborhood and associating with a small circle of acquaintances season after season, year after year. To the undiscerning eye their existence may appear to be nothing more than "a quick succession of busy nothings," but like Austen readers, observant birders notice individuals and their relationships and dramas within any chickadee flock.

As in Austen's world, chickadee flocks have a strict, stable social hierarchy. Chickadees become "marriageable" the spring after their first winter.

As in Austen's world, chickadee flocks have a strict, stable social hierarchy. Chickadees become "marriageable" the spring after their first winter. Those young chickadees start out at the bottom of the social ladder, rising in rank as they get older. Pairs are composed of birds of equal social standing. Elizabeth Bennet could have been a chickadee when she noted about Darcy, "He is a gentleman; I am a gentleman's daughter; so far we are equal."

Female chickadees can't help but look over the neighborhood males, finding the best singers especially attractive. Like Austen characters, a chickadee's "imagination is very rapid; it jumps from admiration to love, from love to matrimony in a moment," but no English heroine would accept mashed-up insects from a lovestruck male. In both worlds, settling love relationships involves drama, but once mate choices are worked out, the dénouement is short and sweet, the consummation private. Some infidelity has always occurred; as Mrs. Bennet might have noted, "I assure you there is quite as much of *that* going on with chickadees as with people." Yet in both cases, lasting bonds endure year after year.

Chickadee romance surges every spring and ebbs every summer. A pair may not seem like a unit in fall and early winter, but one sunny January morning, the male starts singing anew, and his mate listens afresh. He may ask her, like Darcy, "If your feelings are still what they were last April, tell me so at once. My affections and wishes are unchanged." And just like the previous April, and the April before that, their feelings will not be repressed. Chickadees probably cannot fix on which hour, or glance, or words laid the foundation, but for yet another season, they settle into domestic felicity.

It worked in Jane Austen's world, and it works for chickadees today.

AT LAST MY LOVE HAS COME ALONG

Complicated relationship dramas are limited to young chickadees and older chickadees who lost their mate since the previous year. Unlike Colonel Brandon in *Sense and Sensibility*, an unattached older chickadee would more likely court Marianne Dashwood's widowed mother than the beautiful young girl herself.

No English heroine would accept mashed-up insects from a lovestruck male.

BLUE-FOOTED BOOBY

Happy Feet

*I*magine an Irish line dancer who isn't Irish, doesn't like dancing in formation, and refuses to coordinate his steps with anyone else. He doesn't perform for crowds, saving his best moves for an audience of one. And he flashes bright blue footwear with every step. Extraordinarily disciplined, no matter how exuberantly he moves his feet, he keeps his arms straight down, lifting them only for one "sky pointing" display when he raises his bill, wings, and tail straight up. This is the Blue-footed Booby.

The Irish might think him a misfit, but his dance is a hit with the only audience he cares about. He starts by strutting in front of a female, flaunting his blue feet more exuberantly than Elvis ever flaunted his blue suede shoes. Then he presents nest materials with a flourish and again displays those fancy feet. He'll continue to dance through courtship as the female builds the nest and lays two or three eggs, ever wowed and inspired by the brilliance of his feet. The more intense the color, the more fit he is and the more likely their young will thrive.

In most species, two older individuals make the most successful pairs, but oddly enough, the Blue-footed Booby chicks most likely to thrive have parents who are not the same age. An older male or female booby will have

He starts by strutting in front of a female, flaunting his blue feet more exuberantly than Elvis ever flaunted his blue suede shoes.

the best reproductive success if its mate is young, and vice versa. One 2018 study found that nestlings raised by same-age parents, whether both parents are old or young, carry significantly more ticks and other parasites than nestlings of different-age parents.

Blue-footed Boobies are considered monogamous within the breeding season: one male and one female share a nesting territory and parental responsibilities. But they do not have a good track record when it comes to fidelity. When females fly overhead, males, whether or not they already have a mate, often let out shrill whistles. Females aren't quite so demonstrative but, until they start incubating eggs, also engage in occasional hookups. Neither parent demands paternity tests or questions where a particular egg came from. Females incubate their eggs, and both parents feed and protect the young in their nest without fail.

Each can count on the other to fulfill the basic obligations of parenthood, and that's all any booby, male or female, expects or wants from its mate. The exuberance of dancing to show off extravagantly brilliant feet, and the thrill of being an audience of one, are ephemeral joys no booby would deny its partner.

It's not looking for a soul mate. A sole mate is plenty good enough.

UNDER THE SEA

Blue-footed Boobies are found in the eastern Pacific Ocean from California to the Galápagos Islands down into Peru, never coming to land except to breed on rocky coasts. Boobies catch fish by plunge-diving into the ocean from great heights, sometimes more than 100 yards above the water. They hit the water at about 60 miles per hour and can shoot down more than 80 feet below the surface. These divers have a system of large air sacs in the skull to protect their brain from both the impact and water pressure. To keep water out of their respiratory system, their nostrils are sealed off. On land or sea, boobies breathe, and whistle, through the corners of their mouth.

BROWN-HEADED COWBIRD

Are You My Mother?

Twins separated at birth and raised apart often grow up with uncanny similarities. As adults, they often say they felt unmoored, as if knowing there was someone out there that they were supposed to be with.

Brown-headed Cowbirds are "nest parasites," laying their eggs in the nests of other species, so mother cowbirds adopt out their young to different families, of different species, but something deep in their bones tells them from the start that they are cowbirds. As soon as they can feed themselves, they strike out in search of others like them. They may never find their biological parents, and may not recognize them if they do, but they quickly find and join cowbird flocks.

Brown-headed Cowbirds were once tightly associated with nomadic bison on North America's grasslands, feeding on insects stirred up by the giant mammals and in their piles of manure. When bison moved on, the adult cowbirds had to follow or they'd starve. Fortunately they weren't abandoning their nests, because cowbirds don't build nests. Laying their eggs in the nests of species that found food independent of bison ensured that young cowbirds would be cared for whether the parents were there or not.

This isn't to say that mother cowbirds have no maternal instincts. As long as they remain in an area, they seem to keep tabs on nests with their young. When a foster parent recognizes and removes a cowbird egg, sometimes the cowbird destroys the remaining eggs or young and trashes the nest, as if in revenge. There are also records of mother cowbirds fighting predators that were stalking their genetic chicks.

Human foster parents are given a choice. The birds selected to raise cowbird chicks don't get to choose. The female cowbird always tosses out one egg before depositing her own in a nest, and she usually selects a smaller species to raise her progeny. Her eggs develop more quickly than those of other songbirds, hatching sooner, giving each of her chicks a better chance than the remaining young of the foster parents.

Most birds raise at least one or two of their own chicks successfully along with a cowbird, but their production of young goes down significantly in each nest where one of their own eggs has been replaced. Some species such as Black-capped Vireos and Kirtland's Warblers have become endangered because of cowbirds expanding into their limited ranges after people changed the habitat, especially by bringing in cattle.

That's not a baby cowbird's fault, and despite how quickly it grows, it isn't aggressive toward its foster siblings, though it may inadvertently crush tinier nestlings. After it fledges, it depends on its foster parents for another 2 weeks to a month and then flies off to find other cowbirds — without so much as a backward glance at the birds who gave up some of their own young to raise it.

TAKE A BOW

Cowbirds are extremely social, hanging out in huge flocks throughout the year. In spring, males in a flock make charming liquid gurgles while opening their wings and bowing forward, displaying both to each other and to any nearby females. Sometimes a male alights near a female on the ground or a branch or wire, bowing while making a rich gurgle and sidling toward her. She calls the shots, giving full consent or just saying no. He simply picks himself up, dusts himself off, and starts all over again.

Sometimes a male alights near a female, bowing while making a rich gurgle and sidling toward her.

COMMON LOON

Passion in Fresh Water

easide passion may work for humans, plovers, and some other birds, but saltwater does not stir a loon's romantic juices. Until they're on a secluded northern lake with a willing loon of the opposite sex, sparks cannot fly for them. It takes 3 years for most loons to leave the oceans and the Gulf of Mexico to mate.

Loons claim ownership of their territory by staring down competitors with their brilliant eyes and, at night when eyes are hard to see, by the males' yodeling. If a competitor, male or female, ignores those signals, loons come to blows. Most fatal attacks come from underwater, the attacker swimming directly under the opponent and stabbing from beneath. Necropsies of loons reveal that about half have injuries, sometimes long healed, that were inflicted by another loon's bill from underwater. Above-water attacks are less lethal but equally aggressive, the birds jabbing bills and beating each other with their wings.

Older loons who have already nested on a lake have a definite advantage over younger ones, from their track record of winning battles and their intimate knowledge of the territory. Three-year-olds lose virtually every battle. Even as they mature, it's hard to win out against defending adults. The average age for loons to start breeding is 6.

Both male and female engage in these battles every year against newcomers of their own sex. Because experienced birds who already successfully won and held that territory have the advantage, pairs usually end up nesting together year after year. The longest known pairing lasted 11 years. Whether the previous mate or a new loon wins, male and female fall in love just as readily. The winner takes all, but once the pair is formed for the season, loons are entirely faithful — no cases of extra-pair paternity have ever been noted, even in DNA studies of large samples of pairs and their offspring.

When courting, the two make synchronized swimming moves consisting of short dives, circle swimming, and bill dipping. The male selects the nest site, but either mate might make the "come hither" seduction move, swimming toward the nest site while making a series of faint hoots and mews. They mate on land near the nest, continuing with high frequency until their two eggs are laid. Once the honeymoon is over, they share all parental responsibilities.

SMOKE GETS IN YOUR EYES

Hormones both impel loons toward fresh water in spring and turn their eyes brilliant red. That bright color grows dull as a loon's interest in love, family, and territory dissipates for the winter. Soon enough, the birds will regain those passionate eyes of spring.

After the chicks hatch, the parents often fish in different parts of the lake, each with one chick. They continue vocalizing to one another, but now the family, not the pair, is the primary unit. When the chicks can catch their own fish, the adults leave them and each other for the year. Their young can migrate on their own when their wing feathers reach full size, and with the parents gone, they don't have to share a lake's limited supply of fish.

Whether the previous mate or a new loon wins, male and female fall in love just as readily.

EASTERN BLUEBIRD

The Bold and the Beautiful

Dorothy Gale yearned to escape with bluebirds to some-where "Over the Rainbow." Eastern Bluebirds would of course have been living on her farm, but her lonely rest-lessness made Kansas seem dull sepia. She could imagine bluebirds in a Tech-nicolor world, but only "somewhere over the rainbow."

As the phrase "bluebird of happiness" attests, Dorothy isn't the only person who associates bluebirds with happiness. Their voices, as warm and mellow as Judy Garland's, along with the way they perch above their cozy birdhouse and how both parents work so well together to raise their chicks, all contribute to our impressions of domestic bliss.

We humans haven't figured out what bluebird song lyrics mean, but the male's happiness seems to depend on his ability to keep other male bluebirds at bay. During the breeding season when he has or soon will have hungry mouths to feed, he refuses to share his territory.

The male's happiness seems to depend on his ability to keep other male bluebirds at bay.

LOVE THE ONE YOU'RE WITH

When a female wanders off her mate's nesting territory, chances are she'll meet up with another male or two, and chances are she'll come home to lay at least one egg genetically unrelated to her original partner. Some studies show that as many as 25 to 30 percent of all Eastern Bluebird broods are sired by more than one male. The resident male raises the young as if they were all his own. Fortunately for bluebird happiness, they never take paternity tests.

Neighboring males aren't interested just in his food supplies, either. Female bluebirds are no more strictly monogamous than males. We humans haven't figured out what female bluebirds find attractive, but it's almost certainly not movie-star handsomeness. In field and lab studies, when the colors of some males' feathers were brightened or dulled, females didn't seem to care.

It's not just female bluebirds who can't say no to extra-pair mating. If a female wanders onto a mated pair's territory when the resident female is gone, that male responds with enthusiasm. If the visitor doesn't have her own mate, she may even lay an egg in this pair's nest, leaving the resident female to incubate and raise a chick who is not genetically hers.

Birds that nest once a year get all their soap-opera drama over with fairly quickly. A single pair of bluebirds may nest two or three times, so in an area with lots of bluebirds, the drama may be drawn out for months. As summer wanes, though, so does the intensity of raging hormones.

Not coincidentally, so does the number of chicks in later broods — a pair's first nest often contains five or even six eggs, but the last just three or even two. The following year, pairs of bluebirds who successfully raised broods usually get back together. In the world of happy bluebirds, loyalty and hanky-panky are not incompatible.

EASTERN SCREECH-OWL

You're Not Getting Older; You're Getting Better

*H*ow long any animal successfully negotiates life is an indicator of overall fitness and gene quality, so in many species, the older an animal gets, the more attractive it becomes to the opposite sex. In some mammals and overproducing domestic birds, females grow less fertile with age, making maturity seem less alluring than youthfulness. In wild birds, however, the idea that "you're not getting older; you're getting better" is hardly an empty advertising slogan — it's the way birds see it.

In many species, the older an animal gets, the more attractive it becomes to the opposite sex.

Some species give clear signals of increasing age. Cedar Waxwings develop more red wing markings as they get older; hawks called accipiters start out with yellow eyes that grow orange and then deeper and deeper red with age. These birds have what scientists call *assortative mating* — they sort themselves out by age, older birds matched with older mates.

Eastern Screech-Owls also have assortative mating, but how they identify one another's ages is still a mystery, at least for us humans. Young birds start seeking a mate their first winter, when most available birds are also young. But after an older screech owl dies, how does its surviving mate recognize, out of the smaller pool of potential mates, which birds are its age? Only the screech owl knows for sure.

However they find each other, screech owls usually stay together as long as they both live and, based on paternity tests of chicks, they are entirely faithful. Unlike most birds of prey, these couples don't merely tolerate each other. They seem genuinely companionable even outside the breeding season, often roosting in the same hole even during warm spells when sharing body heat isn't important.

PROPERTY RIGHTS

Screech owls defend what is called a *polyterritory*. Rather like wealthy condo owners who maintain multiple apartments, screech owls don't claim rights over the land surrounding their roosting and nesting cavities — just the cavities themselves. A single pair may claim several cavities within a landscape hosting other pairs as well. To make it clear who owns what, screech owls spend time hunting near each of their own cavities and alternate which ones they roost in.

Two mated screech owls sometimes roost apart. Separate sleeping arrangements don't seem to imply that their bond is weaker — just that they both care about guarding their real estate.

The only time they never share the cavity is during the nesting period. The female has all the responsibilities of producing and incubating the eggs as the male hunts for her and his offspring; he sleeps in another cavity for the duration.

To switch off aggression and signal cooperativeness and even friendliness, screech-owl pairs engage in allopreening, tenderly preening each other's facial and head feathers; they also do this with their chicks. Allopreening, and making their trilling call back and forth, seem to cement the bond between mated birds, and both activities take place year-round, even when the birds are least interested in sex.

Other birds who mate for life, especially birds of prey, must rekindle their relationship with their mate each year, with display flights and other courtship activities. Building trust between birds who sport dangerous talons is imperative, but screech owls already know they can trust each other.

Courtship behaviors begin in January or February, when hormones intensify the owls' calling and give it an amorous spin. On a night stroll in the winter woods, we may hear several making their long, plaintive trills.

FLORIDA SCRUB-JAY

Failure to Launch

*M*any species who mate for life, from chickadees to eagles, produce eggs in spring and send off their independent young by summer's end. The pair may stay near each other through the winter, as chickadees do, or take separate winter vacations, as eagles do. Either way, romance is rekindled around anniversary time.

Young geese and cranes stay with their parents through fall and winter, not giving the adults a moment of "alone time." The parents don't get irritated because, by the time those young hatched, the parents' hormonal levels had dropped anyway. But as their anniversary approaches, secure in the knowledge that they've given their young all they need to survive on their own, these parents abruptly decamp, heading back to their secluded nesting territory. They may have been together for 1 year or 20 yet every spring, as soon as they finally escape from the previous year's young, their romantic fires burn just as passionately as they did first time around.

But in one species, parents may nearly always be stuck with young from previous years, making it difficult to have a romantic tryst without curious young eyes following their every move. Florida Scrub-Jays are one of the few birds who don't wander more than a mile or two from their natal territory.

Young females often wander two or three territories away from where they hatched in search of a mate. Their brothers stick with their parents until a male on a nearby territory or their own father dies, or they manage to hammer out a deal for their own bit of real estate near their parents' place. In most years, more than half of all Florida Scrub-Jay families have at least one young male remaining with the parents; that number may rise as high as 80 percent after a good nesting year.

The loss of privacy is offset by the help those young give the pair, feeding the nestlings, defending the nest area against territorial competitors and potential predators, and serving as lookouts for the family. Reproductive success improves with helpers.

Pairs are surprisingly romantic, both males and females offering their mate delicacies to eat.

HOMIES

Florida Scrub-Jays are extraordinary as both homebodies and habitat specialists, limited to oak scrub. They can fly as well as other birds but are extremely reluctant to do so over unfamiliar habitats. As scrub habitat disappears in Florida, pathways between scrub-jay population centers have disappeared. Over time, this isolation of the Atlantic Coast, central Florida, and southwestern Florida populations has led the groups, separated by less than 100 miles, to develop different vocalizations.

As a rule, ravens, crows, and jays seem to need more privacy than most birds. Florida Scrub-Jay pairs are surprisingly romantic, both males and females offering their mate delicacies to eat and getting a bit of alone time while sharing sentinel duties. But as we might expect with any parents whose 1-year-old doggedly trails them, opportunities to have sex are limited. Florida Scrub-Jays steal intimate moments at the nest when their helpers are off eating or serving as sentinels.

As in any romantic comedy, roadblocks standing in the way of intimacy somehow fan the attraction. Perhaps that's why the fidelity of Florida Scrub-Jay pairs is so high. Whether their courtship ends with a literal "Till death do us part" vow or not, nearly all pairs live up to that standard, and their faithfulness to one another is absolute. There has never been a single documented case of extra-pair paternity in the species.

Florida Scrub-Jay plumage is true blue; designers of wedding and anniversary cards couldn't find a better symbol of fidelity and enduring love.

GREAT BLUE HERON

Say It with Sticks

Most large wading birds have an easy time finding potential partners; their most difficult task is selecting the right one.

As with many mammals and birds, it's the male Great Blue Heron who invites the female on that all-important first date. A human male will often "say it with flowers." Expensive arrangements may indicate that he has enough riches to support a home and family. His willingness to squander it on flowers, however, would make any sensible heron question his sanity when he could much more easily and affordably give something useful: sticks.

Offering a stick stirs romantic feelings in both birds; after putting it in place in the nest, the pair often mate.

Great Blue Herons stay focused on the end game. Will this in fact be a mate who understands what is involved in settling down and raising a family? First, two birds signal their interest. The male extends his neck, raises his bill vertically, and erects his neck plumes; then the female erects the plumes on her head, neck, and breast while lowering her head and clapping her bill to make snapping sounds. All this proclaims their health and physical qualities.

Then they decide whether to build a new nest or refurbish an old one. Most herons nest in colonies, each pair refurbishing an unoccupied nest from a previous year or selecting a new nest site.

Now it's time to get down to business. One by one, the male picks up broken sticks from the ground, or breaks them off standing trees, and carries them to the female at the nest site. She stretches her neck toward him and accepts each offering. The act of transferring a stick stirs romantic feelings in both birds; after putting it in place in the nest, the pair often mate. Females seldom reject sticks — even a small or weirdly shaped one can be placed somewhere in the bulky construction. To turn one down would damage the delicate bond between the mates.

The male continues to bring sticks as eggs are being laid and then incubated, cementing the pair's attachment and making the nest even sturdier. In 2012, a nest cam at the Cornell Lab of Ornithology's Sapsucker Woods tracked every movement of a nesting pair, revealing that every time the female laid an egg and showed it to the male, he flew off, brought her a new stick, and they mated all over again. Those two herons mated many dozens of times during the weeks of nest construction and egg production, but after the final egg was laid, both birds seemed immediately to lose interest in sex. Having a complete clutch of eggs changed their focus to parenthood

Once the clutch was complete, both birds lost interest in sex. They settled down to parenthood, taking turns incubating the eggs and then brooding and feeding the young. It could have been a Great Blue Heron who wrote that there is a season and a time for every purpose under heaven. Of course, the heron would have also added sticks.

YOU ARE SO BEAUTIFUL

Both male and female Great Blue Herons want a mate with showy *nuptial plumage* — long, soft, flowing feathers rising from the head, throat, and back. They also consider how green the skin is between the eyes and bill, and how pink the legs are. These specialized feathers and the brightness of the skin are good indicators of a bird's health and ability to obtain nutritious food. Beautiful breeding plumage may also appeal to a bird's aesthetic sensibilities, though no one has yet interviewed herons to confirm.

GREAT HORNED OWL

Be My Valentine

*I*n February, most northern birds have retreated south or focus on survival. They spend the short days finding food to keep their metabolic furnace burning on the long, frozen nights. But Cupid's arrow finds one receptive target on Valentine's Day.

Great Horned Owls, found almost everywhere in North America and even into Central and South America, tend to mate for life and are usually nonmigratory. Those in the Southwest are as well adapted to dry desert heat as those in the Canadian prairies are to subzero temperatures and deep snow. Southeastern birds start nesting in January or even December, and desert birds may wait until closer to the monsoon season — but northern ones find romance around Valentine's Day.

Nicknamed "feathered tigers" for their color, ferocity, and catlike yellow eyes, these solitary hunters usually keep some distance from their mate while staying in vocal contact. But when their romantic energy builds up, hooting isn't enough, and they start roosting side by side, especially when they select a nest site.

The much larger female can hurt the male if she rebuffs him, so his every movement during courtship is designed to please her. He bows and hoots as he sidles toward her, cocking his tail and inflating his throat to make his white bib appear huge.

When she calls back encouragingly, he cautiously draws even closer, bobbing his tail. Then they both start bowing toward each other with wings drooped, inflating their white bibs (which show up beautifully in darkness) and bobbing their tails in synchrony, occasionally pausing to gently nuzzle each other. High-pitched giggling, screaming, and bill snapping lead to mating, both birds hooting throughout the act.

> *When their romantic energy builds up, hooting isn't enough.*

The female lays one to five eggs anywhere from a day to a week apart; the pair mates frequently until the clutch is complete. The male delivers food throughout the night so she never has to leave the nest; to poop, she just backs up and shoots it away. One female was observed leaving her nest to help her mate drive off another male from their territory. Her eggs, unattended for 20 minutes when the temperature was 13 degrees below zero Fahrenheit (−25° Celsius), hatched successfully.

The male provides food throughout the time the chicks are dependent, a good month or two after they fledge. The female is the one who tears prey apart and feeds the young. She'll also brood her growing family until the chicks can maintain their body temperature. The parents' Valentine's Day romance gives the young owls a big boost when they start learning how to hunt. They're old enough to practice on all the inexperienced baby mammals emerging in early summer.

Most owlets remain at least somewhat dependent through midsummer, linger on or near the parents' territory until November or December, and only then strike out on their own. Their parents spend the darkest evenings of the year focused on their own needs, but by Valentine's Day, Cupid will strike again.

COZY UP

The female's large size gives her plenty of body heat to share. Even when air temperatures are double digits below zero, she can press the hot, bare skin of her belly — her brood patch — against the eggs to keep them a toasty 100 degrees Fahrenheit (37.7° Celsius). It takes a minimum of 30 days for the eggs to start hatching.

HERRING GULL

Across a Crowded Room

*I*magine a young couple just starting out, looking for their first home. They find a huge apartment complex not far from (and similar to) the homes they knew as children. The units are easily affordable, and if lacking in amenities (such as a roof or walls between apartments), the complex seems like a happenin' place in a richly diverse neighborhood. The male does most of the house hunting. As soon as he finds a nice little vacancy, he runs it by his mate, she approves, and they move right in. They don't even need to fork over a security deposit.

Our young couple happen to be Herring Gulls. Management insists that all units be occupied by mated pairs, though they do allow some males to claim a territory provisionally. The homeowners' association caters to diversity: residents include a few other species of gulls, as well as terns, oceanic diving birds, and cormorants. The tenants of our gulls' unit the previous year were a same-sex pair of Herring Gulls. The two females successfully raised two chicks after finding a willing sperm donor, but a Peregrine Falcon nabbed one mother over the winter, opening the vacancy.

The lack of walls means our two lovers don't get any privacy at all, but there's an unwritten rule that everyone minds their own business. Whether it's due to self-consciousness or not, Herring Gulls don't have any displays only about courtship. When she wants to mate, our female approaches her male making the head-tossing display — exactly what chicks do when begging for food. Perhaps this is similar to human couples using baby talk in their private banter. Both Herring Gulls toss their heads like this just before mating. Whether their neighbors avert their eyes hasn't been studied.

> *When she wants to mate, our female approaches her male making the head-tossing display — exactly what chicks do when begging for food.*

Privacy isn't nearly as important to Herring Gulls as security is. Without walls between units or a lockable door, and no written leases to make ownership clear, our young couple must spend much of their courtship and honeymoon making sure no one breaks in and takes over their little home. That

means no dates: while one is dining out, the other stays home. Their worst problems are with larger gulls, but an efficient neighborhood-watch program enlists the help of neighbors when a Great Black-backed Gull or other dangerous predator approaches.

Unfortunately, some of the most helpful neighbors in that defense can be equally aggressive in trying to enlarge their own territory. Worse, neighbors sometimes eat unattended eggs. They virtually never eat chicks but do peck to death youngsters who toddle through invisible walls between territories, so parents must be ever vigilant.

Herring Gulls often live well into their twenties, and the vast majority stay paired as long as they both shall live. In one long-term study in Newfoundland tracking more than 300 pairs, only eight cases of "divorce" were ever noted.

Our Herring Gull couple first came together a few weeks ago, in late winter, as part of a large flock. One enchanted evening, the male saw a stranger across their crowded pier. He flew to her side and made her his own; now all through their lives they won't dream all alone.

NEIGHBORHOOD WATCH

In many coastal areas of North America and Europe, large sea ducks called Common Eiders always nest within colonies of Herring Gulls. The gulls do take some eider eggs, but their neighborhood-watch programs protect the eiders from predation by eagles and larger, more predaceous gulls.

HOUSE WREN

Singing Casanova

House Wrens believe so fervently in lasting commitments that each male and female makes several every season. Pairs split when their chicks fledge. Usually it's the female who flies off to rest and make a new commitment to a new mate. The remaining parent, usually the male, stays with the fledglings, but he's hardly emotionally scarred by her abandonment. He's too busy falling in love all over again, too. Their young, in turn, will as adults enter into traditional House Wren marriages — faithful for exactly the amount of time that House Wrens are faithful.

He's hardly emotionally scarred by her abandonment. He's too busy falling in love all over again, too.

Male House Wrens seem to throw every fiber of their being into their rich, bubbly songs. Their whole third-of-an-ounce body pulsates with the effort as if the microscopic syrinx within their throat can't possibly produce such volume and exuberance on its own. Each male knows every nook and cranny of his territory, stuffing suitable cavities and crevices with sticks, marking them as his own and also serving to block nest thieves and predators from breaking in.

The number of sticks and their arrangement seem haphazard, but they form a platform with a depression perfect for the female to fill with a cup nest. This literal Casanova (*casa nova* means "new house" in Venetian Italian) uses these housing units to invite females to come nest with him. If one approaches, he starts squeaking his sales pitch, faster and faster, the squeaks becoming continuous if she actually enters a house.

She may mate with one or two males before making up her mind, so some of the first eggs may have been fathered by a male other than her final choice. Once she seals the deal by building the soft nest where she'll deposit her eggs, the male can relax for a bit.

A female's interest in sex with her mate dwindles while she's incubating, even as he keeps singing. His songs reassure her of his good health and focus even as her mind is starting to wander farther afield, noticing males in surrounding territories. The male also sings to alert his mate and their offspring when he approaches with food.

CLEAN BREAK

Human parents generally live year-round with the same mate and maintain ties with their children throughout their lives. House Wren young seldom return close to the territory where they grew up, and after they disperse there is no evidence that they recognize their parents, or vice versa. Moving away from their natal territories may help prevent parent-offspring matings.

For the first 5 or 6 days after the eggs hatch, the mother spends most of her time keeping the chicks warm while the father provides most of their meals. All that work may be what prompts the female to leave the family. They share feeding duties more equally during the next week or 10 days, until the young leave the nest. Producing a second batch is easier if she skips the last grueling week or two of provisioning fledglings. She can recharge her batteries by moseying off and, while on vacation, looking for a new Casanova.

The bonds between House Wren mates may seem tenuous, but they last exactly as long as they need to.

LAYSAN ALBATROSS

When I'm Sixty-Four

*I*n 1967, the Beatles released the song "When I'm Sixty-Four," to the almost universal delight of 16-year-old humans. But one female Laysan Albatross, at least 16 years old herself that year, did not notice.

That albatross, nicknamed "Wisdom," was still alive and well as of 2019. She was trapped and banded on Midway Island in 1956, when Paul McCartney was 14. Scientists called her a "nesting adult" but had no way of knowing how old she was beyond the fact that albatrosses are at least 5 years old when they begin nesting (the vast majority are 8 or 9 years old). Wisdom couldn't have hatched any later than 1951, and she was almost certainly at least a year or two older than that. We'll never know — she has no birth certificate.

Like the Beatles, albatrosses spend much of their life on the road, or at least out at sea, without their mate. Unlike some human musicians, albatrosses maintain their commitment to their mate even during those long absences.

Every November, after spending months wandering alone over the open ocean, Wisdom returns to Midway. She may be wondering if her mate will show up but has no doubt that, if still alive, he'll still need her. Unlike Paul

McCartney, Wisdom never wonders if her mate will still feed her — courtship for albatrosses involves elaborate dancing but never wining and dining.

Courtship for albatrosses involves elaborate dancing but never wining and dining.

Even during the weeks when they are most intimately focused on each other and their shared parental responsibilities, albatrosses take turns heading out to sea to eat as the other keeps the home fires burning. When the satiated mate returns, they greet each other with affectionate bill touching and dancing, cementing their warm bond without sharing food. Soon enough, the hungry mate sets off in search of his or her own squid.

Steadfastness defines the albatross character. Unlike fickle humans who jump in and out of fads with astonishing frequency, albatrosses honor the traditions of their parents, grandparents, and great-grandparents. In 2019, when Wisdom

THE LONG AND WINDING ROAD

The scientist who originally banded Wisdom in 1956, Chandler Robbins, returned to Midway Island in 2002 to band albatrosses again. Leg bands don't last many years on birds exposed to so much saltwater. When he replaced the band on her leg, he painstakingly went through years of banding cards to find out when that band was originally put on. It was also a replacement band, so he tracked down the number of the one it replaced.

One by one, he went through decades of banding cards until he discovered that he himself put the original band on Wisdom almost a half century earlier. This set the longevity record for Laysan Albatrosses, and for *all* wild birds, and made national news. That's when the name "Wisdom" was first given to her.

was at least 68 years old, she was using the exact same romantic moves she had perfected well before the Beatles era. She has danced the same way, year after year, even as the twist, disco, break dancing, line dancing, and hip-hop swept the human world. Her moves include bill touching, fanning her wing, and pointing her bill at the sky.

Year after year, she performs her romantic ritual with the same passion and exuberance as she did decades ago. And year after year, something in the way she moves attracts her mate like no other lover.

LIMPKIN

The Food of Love

A popular delicacy with a French name, escargot (meaning "edible snail") is traditionally made with large European land snails. A diet of snails may seem unappetizing to people without gourmet tastes, and apple snails from the Americas haven't been well received by European palates, but it turns out they make the perfect aphrodisiac for one handsome all-American bird, the Limpkin.

This relative of cranes, the only member of the family Aramidae, lives in wetlands from Florida to northern Argentina, specializing on apple snails, supplemented with freshwater mussels, a few other snails, insects, frogs, lizards, and worms. The Limpkin bill is such an extraordinary tool, wielded so expertly, that it takes a mere 10 to 20 seconds to extract a soft snail body from its perfectly undamaged shell.

Variety may be the spice of life, but apple snails are the way to a female Limpkin's heart. A lonely male makes a loud *kow* call, hoping to lure a nearby unattached female to his territory. To keep her there, he must impress her with the big, juicy innards of an apple snail. She's perfectly capable of getting her own food, but apparently culinary gifts from a male taste better and heighten her romantic impulses.

Once the pair bond forms, the two are fairly inseparable as they feed, work on their nest, and produce five or so eggs. When the clutch is complete, they take turns incubating. To keep their pair bond strong throughout this whole time, the male continues to give her snails, often followed by sex. That is more than enough to keep most females at their mates' side, but one female tracked by researchers wandered off her mate's territory for an hour each day to accept a tasty snail from an unpaired male, and thanked him with a roll in the hay or, more precisely, in the marsh vegetation.

To keep their pair bond strong throughout this whole time, the male continues to give her snails, often followed by sex.

SLOW FOOD MOVEMENT

When the native apple snail of Florida, which feeds on rotted plant and animal matter, became badly endangered, Limpkins and another specialist, the Snail Kite, were endangered as well. Another large snail, the channeled apple snail native to South America, escaped into Florida via the aquarium and pet trade. It eats healthy vegetation, wreaking such havoc with the Florida Everglades ecosystem that it's considered one of the worst invasive species in the world. Neither Limpkins nor Snail Kites consult field guides before eating, and apparently apple snails all taste pretty much the same to them, so both are thriving now.

With few such exceptions, most Limpkin pairs are monogamous from the time a female accepts snails from her male until their young are feeding without adult help. Some females desert their family earlier, especially if the pair lost some or most of their brood — which would indicate overall food shortages in the area. Lack of adequate food means that the mother needs more time than usual to recover from egg production. Sometimes both parents remain with the chicks for a month or more, but often it's the male who finishes off their education.

As soon as the eggs hatch, the male stops feeding the female. Without those feedings, and as their hormonal urges settle down, the pair loses interest in each other except as co-parents.

Some pairs reunite the following spring, but most form new attachments, perhaps honoring the motto "First come, first served." The first to be served a succulent snail becomes the literal first mate, at least for that year.

MALLARD

Going Steady

*M*any junior high kids seem to think their first venture into romance may last a lifetime. In contrast, when a young female Mallard is first courted by mobs of males vying for her approval, she's already a hard-beaked realist. Mallards don't mate for life, but a good temporary mate provides a female with a few advantages, including social status and help when other drakes get irritating. This may be all she needs from a male.

Starting in fall, Mallard drakes surround lone swimming females to perform the "head shake," "head flick," and "swimming shake." Up to five males coordinate their displays into synchronized bursts of activity, grunting and putting their tails up or down simultaneously. Unlike humans, female Mallards cannot roll their eyes.

Fortunately, each female quickly finds a male interesting enough to encourage. Older males and those with the best-quality plumage are in highest demand, likely to pass their superior genes on to their offspring. Females are especially drawn to their most dogged suitors — after all, males distracted by other females during courtship are most likely to wander when things get

Older males and those with the best-quality plumage are in highest demand.

serious, too. A Mallard hen needs her mate close during the pair's honeymoon, when she's building the nest and laying eggs.

Each morning, the pair visits the nest for anywhere from a few minutes to an hour. The female adds a few nesting materials, lays an egg, and covers the clutch with a downy blanket. Duty done, the pair spends the rest of the day focused on their honeymoon, which is marked with plenty of love in the afternoon. Either male or female may initiate sex with a head-pumping display; the other matches the display to show willingness.

Mallards produce an average of eight eggs in a clutch (sometimes as many as twelve or even thirteen) in 2 to 3 weeks. Both birds stay focused on sex during that time to ensure that each egg will be fertilized.

After the last egg is laid and the female starts incubating, she loses interest in sex. An extremely devoted male may stick around for a week or more, but incubating females don't need help, and colorful males may even present a hazard, attracting predators. Fortunately, males also lose interest in sex as their bodies prepare to molt into fresh plumage. They join convivial flocks of other bachelor fathers, leaving child-rearing to the professionals.

The following winter, regardless of age and experience, Mallards fall back into high school mode, each getting a clean start with a new temporary mate. It's just ducky.

MADE FOR EACH OTHER

Unlike most male birds, drakes have more than a simple "cloacal protuberance" that meets the female's cloaca during mating. In breeding readiness, male Mallards have a corkscrew-shaped penis-like organ that emerges during mating. It can be shockingly long: up to 8 inches, or more than a third of their body length.

The female's oviduct (the pathway for sperm to fertilize eggs and for the egg to exit the body) is long and twisted, often with blind offshoots that can sequester an unwanted male's sperm before it reaches the ovum. The shape of the oviduct may change during courtship and early mating (before males are producing sperm) to fit the unique shape of her selected mate's penis.

NORTHERN CARDINAL

Romantic Duets

*I*n the musical *Oklahoma!* Laurey and Curly finally admit their love with the beautiful and stirring reprise of "People Will Say We're in Love." Northern Cardinals also announce their loving commitment with stirring duets.

As if living in a Rodgers and Hammerstein universe, mated cardinals often communicate in song. Sitting on the nest, a female may sing out to her distant mate that everything is all right, or that she's a bit hungry. Her songs are longer and more complex than his, but she sings only through courtship and the breeding season. Male cardinals make up in quantity what they lack in nuance, singing year-round.

> *As if living in a Rodgers and Hammerstein universe, mated cardinals often communicate in song.*

In show business and in the world of cardinals, even the best singing doesn't guarantee faithfulness. About 20 percent of cardinal pairings end in "divorce," and even when pairs stick together, anywhere from 9 to 35 percent of nestlings are fathered by a different male than their siblings are. Female

THROUGH THE LOOKING GLASS

Both male and female cardinals attack their reflection in people's windows, due in large part to the fact that reflections cannot sing. Cardinals sing to establish and defend their territory. When a cardinal can't hear a single challenger yet keeps seeing an upstart in a window, raising his or her crest in a display of aggression, it's endlessly distressing. The more aggressively a cardinal fights that perceived intruder, the more aggressively the reflection fights back.

Covering the window on the outside with screening or paper until the cardinal gets busy with nesting solves the problem. The quicker we do this, the less likely the cardinal is to get so fixated that it obsessively checks out other windows looking for that silent, invincible competitor.

cardinals are territorial against other females, possibly to keep competitors from distracting their mates.

Both birds select the nest site, but the female does the majority of nest construction, the male often bringing materials for her to use. Males occasionally sit on eggs but don't have an incubation patch and may not hunker down against the eggs as incubating females do.

For the first 2 or 3 days after the eggs hatch, the female may spend her entire days and nights brooding them, but that responsibility eases off as the nestlings start maintaining their own body temperature. During any hours that a nest is exposed to direct sunlight, the female may stand above the nestlings to shade them.

Meanwhile, the male feeds the young more often than she does. She can take up the slack if something happens to him, but cardinal chicks have their best chance of survival in two-parent households.

In well-functioning pairs, the male takes all the responsibility for fledglings about 12 days after they leave the nest as the female starts a new nest. That first batch will be entirely independent by the time the new eggs hatch, when Dad will transfer his attention to them.

When adult pairs stay together through the entire breeding season, they can produce as many as four broods of young in a single season. Some pairs remain together on their breeding territory year-round; others join flocks for the winter. If duets are part of the tie that binds them through nesting, it's the male's singing that keeps them together the rest of the year.

NORTHERN MOCKINGBIRD

Othello Didn't Have to End That Way

Shakespeare's Othello earned the love of Desdemona by regaling her with stories about his thrilling adventures in faraway places. Male Northern Mockingbirds may not read Shakespeare but manage to use Othello's strategy to attract their own mates.

The mockingbird song is a long string of imitations of the sounds they've heard, including those produced by birds and other animals, machines, cell phones, screaming children, and much more, each imitation repeated three or more times. Males may have more than 200 distinct phrases in their repertoire, and new song types are added throughout a male's life.

Why do they make all these imitations? They might be saying, "Listen! I survived this chain saw! Listen! I've mastered cell phones! Listen! I held my own against a big dog! Listen! I've done well on territories near Wood Thrushes! Listen! I faced a lawn mower!"

Whatever the meaning, females are drawn to males with the widest variety of imitations, which may indicate which ones learn and innovate best, or which have the most life experiences. Singing for extended periods also shows how fit and strong they are. Walt Whitman romantically suggested that mockingbirds singing all night long are mourning their lost mates. Although ornithologists shy away from thoughts of birds grieving, they have established that males singing all night do not have a mate, making Whitman at least partially correct.

MOCKINGBIRD'S LAMENT

In *Leaves of Grass*, Walt Whitman wrote a long, sentimental poem about a mockingbird a mockingbird singing all night. "Out of the Cradle Endlessly Rocking" is a fascinating poetic attempt to capture both the rhythm and meaning of a mockingbird's all-night song. A few lines:

> O throat! O throbbing heart!
> And I singing uselessly, uselessly
>   all the night.
> O past! O happy life! O songs of joy!
> In the air, in the woods, over fields,
> Loved! loved! loved! loved! loved!
> But my mate no more, no more
>   with me!
> We two together no more.

The male sings and performs a flight display throughout courtship as he constructs several nest foundations. The female listens as she selects one nest foundation to line with softer grasses, rootlets, and other small fibers, lays the eggs, and incubates them. Her Othello even whispers songs to her during the act of mating.

For all their musical wooing, males aren't big on practical gifts such as food, so the female takes breaks from incubating every quarter or half hour to forage. When the eggs hatch, both parents feed the nestlings about equally, with the female also responsible for keeping them warm. Both parents defend the nestlings from predators, the male taking the larger role in that. The nestlings fledge from the nest when about 12 days old; it takes another week for them to fly well. Both parents continue to feed them for at least a few days. If the pair re-nests, the mother starts focusing on the new nest as the father continues to support the fledglings.

Mockingbird pair bonds usually last as long as both birds survive. They don't pay attention to rumors of infidelity, and although there are a few cases of an egg in a brood fathered by a male other than the female's mate, not one mockingbird has ever smothered his mate with a pillow in a jealous rage. If only William Shakespeare had listened to the mockingbird, he might have given his play a happier ending.

The male sings and performs a flight display throughout courtship as he constructs several nest foundations.

PIPING PLOVER

Love on the Beach

*P*assion on the beach, romanticized in *From Here to Eternity*, seldom works so beautifully in real life. Crowds of people, gobs of seaweed, and sands blackened by tar and oil stymie romance. Gritty sand is unpleasant enough in our hair and eyes, much less our nether regions.

Piping Plovers live out their entire lives on beaches, exposed to the elements and prying eyes. They elude danger thanks to *cryptic* (i.e., concealing) coloration. When pursued, they run a bit and hunker down. Poof! They seem to disappear.

In early spring, males arrive on nesting beaches before females to claim territories above the high tide line. They defend their little plot of sand against competing plovers, other shorebirds, and gulls. They may appear soft and gentle, but these feisty competitors charge even much larger opponents in a horizontal posture, wings raised, body feathers puffed.

When females arrive, each male coaxes prospective mates to his territory with a flight display, beating his wings slowly and deeply as he tilts his body back and forth. If an interested female approaches, he struts on the sand, tossing aside shell fragments and pebbles. Every now and then he stops, squats, and leans forward on his breast, pivoting left and right and kicking sand backward with his feet, leaving a little depression in the sand. He produces several of these "scrapes." Warming up to him, the female may make a few as well.

The pair mates in some of the depressions as if testing out mattresses. When they select the one where the female will deposit the eggs, the honeymoon begins. Some pairs, like human beachcombers, collect bits of shells or pebbles to line the scrapes; others leave the sandy depression as it is. The birds mate over and over every day for a week or longer as she lays her four eggs.

If an interested female approaches, he struts on the sand, tossing aside shell fragments and pebbles.

Unless it's cold, plovers don't start incubating until the third egg is laid. Both seem to lose interest in sex for the season after there are four eggs unless disaster strikes and they must start anew. For 4 weeks, both parents take turns incubating, seldom leaving eggs unattended. The off-duty mate may wander to feed near the water but quickly returns to chase off predators or competitors approaching the territory.

Within hours of hatching, chicks become tiny fluff balls of agitated motion, running helter-skelter over the beach until a magnetic force draws them suddenly back to Mom or Dad. They crowd together to rest and warm up before running off again. They can feed themselves the first day out of the egg but need a parent's body heat and protection for a few weeks — until they become masters of their own fate, taking on the world from here to eternity.

SEASIDE PARENTING

In movies and in the world of Piping Plovers, romance on the beach seldom leads to a lifelong commitment. Piping Plovers have been known to live more than 17 years, but there are no guarantees that the mate from the previous year will still be alive the following year, so perhaps it's a mercy that they don't seek out a "one and only" mate. As often as not, even the most devoted pair selects new partners the following year. That's love and life on the beach.

GREATER PRAIRIE-CHICKEN

Speed Dating

In the search for a compatible partner, some people engage in a ritual called "speed dating." At a pre–planned site they meet various individuals, each for a specific time length (often 3 to 8 minutes). When time is up, everyone moves on to the next candidate. At the end of the meetup, if two parties want to get together, the organizers provide them with contact information.

This concept may seem modern, but one version of speed dating was developed many millennia ago by several species of prairie grouse, including Greater and Lesser Prairie-Chickens, Greater and Gunnison Sage-Grouse, and Sharp-tailed Grouse. Early every spring, birds of both sexes gather at a common area (called a *lek*) in hopes of finding matches. Grouse don't have organizers: birds exchange their own contact information, and body fluids, right there on the lek. Grouse-style speed dating might not be useful for humans looking for romance.

When not dancing or displaying, male grouse are quiet and subdued, garbed in earth tones. They are, however, shape shifters. Like Bruce Banner transforming into the Incredible Hulk right before our eyes, male grouse can inflate brilliantly colored air sacs and erect showy feathers to impress females (and one another) on the lek. The Hulk is unique among humans, but every adult male grouse can transform himself in this way.

During speed-dating encounters, grouse don't discuss their interests, careers, or religious and political beliefs. Each female cares only about how showy each Hulk's feathers and air sacs are, and how well he can dance. Each male competes on those grounds.

Each female quietly rewards her choice and takes off, returning to the lek every day or two during the weeks she's laying eggs. She'll start all over if a predator should take her eggs or chicks, nearly always making the same choice as long as that Number One male survives.

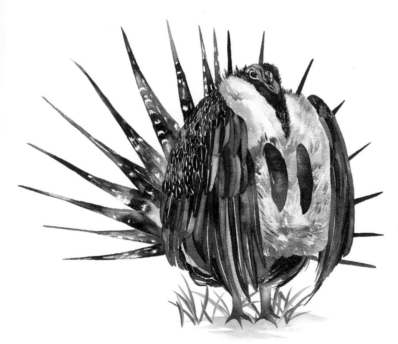

GREATER SAGE-GROUSE

Each female cares only about how showy each Hulk's feathers and air sacs are, and how well he can dance.

Despite the constant rejection, the many unchosen males don't seem to get discouraged. They show up every morning and evening, revved up and ready to dance. And mercifully, they seem entirely focused on one another and on perfecting their posture and form rather than on the females who come through the dating line.

The strongest and most persistent will pass their genes on to the next generation that year. The ones who don't give up but stay in the ring may outlast them, this season or next. And even those who never get chosen throw themselves into the dance without grousing about it. It's a system that works, at least if you're a grouse.

A DISCERNING EYE

To us, displaying males seem identical, but female grouse are more discerning. They make their rounds and then invariably choose the same one or two males, who may father all the young grouse in that area that year. This would simplify paternity test results, if grouse should ever request them.

RED KNOT

The Inconstant Moon

Shakespeare's Juliet called the moon inconstant, but moon phases and tides have been predictable for eons. Just as regular is the emergence of an invertebrate roughly the size and shape of a dinner platter, the horseshoe crab. Migratory movements of the Red Knot, a plump, rust-colored shorebird, are so tied to those rhythms that when knots pair off, they could literally be said to be mooning over each other.

Most birds use many different stopover sites for resting and replenishing their bodies between wintering and breeding grounds. But as tides are peaking every May, the vast majority of Red Knots gravitate to tiny Delaware Bay, ready for a feast during the brief window of time when their best possible food resource is amazingly abundant.

Horseshoe crabs aren't crabs at all: they're more closely related to spiders and ticks. They spend much of their lives at sea, from the soft sandy or muddy bottoms of coastal waters out to the continental shelf. They come ashore to spawn in the sands of the intertidal zone during the highest monthly tides from spring through autumn.

For millions of years, millions of horseshoe crabs produced billions of eggs on the beaches of Delaware Bay. Red Knots adopted a "jump migration" strategy, traveling as much as 5,000 miles without stopping en route to and from Delaware Bay every year. What could be a better source of nutrition than billions of horseshoe crab eggs right there in the sand? That enormous pig-out not only gets the Knots in condition to finish their final long leg of migration, but it also provides the nutrition females need to produce three or four eggs.

Male Knots leave the feast a few days before females to claim a territory on the tundra, scraping out a few possible nest sites on the permafrost. Older birds tend to return to the same site as the year before. When each female is done gorging, she races north and quickly settles in with a male. She selects one of his prepared nest-scrapes and within a few days lays the first egg.

Egg production after a long migration is hard on many tundra-nesting shorebirds, but thanks to the rich food resources in Delaware Bay, Red Knots can be more egalitarian. Males and females have identical plumage, and both bear incubation patches. While one bird incubates the eggs, the other joins a feeding flock in a nearby wetland; then they swap.

Thanks to the rich food resources in Delaware Bay, Red Knots can be more egalitarian. Males and females have identical plumage, and both bear incubation patches.

Due to the effort of producing eggs, females still need more time than males to prepare for their arduous migration, so females may leave the family a few days or even hours after the chicks hatch. No one knows whether the pair somehow communicates a plan to reunite or if they even think about the next year while dealing with the here-and-now urgency of daily life. Whether or not they anticipate it, when next spring's full moon draws them northward, they'll find love again

THE DINOSAUR CONNECTION

Fossils of horseshoe crabs have been found in rocks from 450 million years ago, so they were already an old species when *Tyrannosaurus rex* and *Brontosaurus* walked the land. Considering that most evolutionary biologists see birds as a direct branch of theropod dinosaurs, and that some dinosaurs may well have been feasting on horseshoe crabs or their eggs 65 million years ago, it's fun to think about a modern dinosaur still honoring that old tradition.

RED-WINGED BLACKBIRD

One Big Happy Family

One of the most reliable signs of spring in northern marshes is the arrival of Red-winged Blackbirds, usually just before the ice breaks up. *Okalee!* one yells out from an old cattail, and a dozen others shout back, all opening their wings and erecting their red shoulder feathers in testosterone-fueled displays of masculine prowess. Chases and fights characterize the disputes, as each bird tries to claim as much territory as possible.

Males who hatched the previous year, still looking like females with just a few scattered red shoulder feathers, aren't taken seriously. They seldom get attacked, but neither can they claim a territory, and females ignore them. Land ownership and sex are for adults only.

These young ones who survived the winter are lucky, though. Adults banish immature birds to the periphery of winter feeding and roosting flocks where they are more vulnerable to predation. They spend the new breeding season watching how the big boys manage. The following year they'll remember some lessons and will also have passed the test of winter survival twice, boosting their attractiveness to females.

In early spring, little food is available on still-frozen marshes, so males may spend less than an hour displaying before they all disappear to nearby fields to forage. While they're feeding, they usually keep their epaulets hidden to minimize squabbling — they can't help an aggressive response when they see red, even away from their territories.

As more food becomes available in the marsh, males remain there longer each day. By the time females return, males are spending the whole day in the marsh, each ready to sing *Okalee!* with his wings open, epaulets boldly exposed, to catch each new female's eye. Females settle on territories quickly, without a lot of fanfare. Nearly half of the older females returning from the previous year go straight to the male holding the territory where they nested before.

When a male attracts a mate, he doesn't settle in with her, not while more females are arriving each day. Many females gravitate to the same high-ranking males, or at least their territories. Most males who establish a territory end up with more than one mate, some attracting as many as 15. Ornithologists call these collections of female red-wings "harems," but females are no more faithful to one mate than males are. About half of all red-wing nests contain at least one chick fathered by a male other than the mother's mate.

About half of all red-wing nests contain at least one chick fathered by a male other than the mother's mate.

Females who arrive first in spring start nesting more quickly than later arrivals. Even as one female starts incubating eggs, temporarily losing interest in sex, her mate stays busy with other females. After her first brood fledges or she loses her nest to a predator or a storm, she quickly gets back into breeding mode, too.

Males who grab for all they can get take on enormous responsibilities. Those who amass the biggest territories and attract the most mates work overtime servicing females, chasing away potential predators, defending the boundaries of their territories, and finding food for nestfuls of young.

MIXING IT UP

Both males and females assume a crouch pose, fluttering their wings, to solicit sex. Males mainly approach their own mates for sex, but they're happy to oblige when other males' mates come along and crouch to solicit an assignation. Females squabble among themselves but don't seem to object when other females approach their mate. Broods of chicks with multiple fathers have a higher survival rate than those sharing just one dad. With so much genetic mixing, it's really all just one big happy family.

ROCK PIGEON

Sex and the City

When Carrie Bradshaw wrote her "Sex and the City" column on the eponymous television show, she focused on people, ignoring the great many other New Yorkers out there, naked as jaybirds, engaging in sex in the city where anyone could see.

People living in a city of about 8 million enjoy a certain anonymity. Apparently New York's roughly 7 million pigeons are even more anonymous, living among us while keeping their love lives at least a little private, if only because we tend to ignore them when they're not right at our feet, mooching food.

You'd think Carrie, perched above her Manolo Blahnik spiked heels, would have noticed upscale pigeons wearing their signature red soles, but she didn't. Those red feet are hardly a selling point when just about every pigeon, male and female, has them. If not their designer shoes, how do these birds select lifetime mates out of so many possibilities? People have pondered this question for centuries without definitive answers.

Some studies have found that pigeons prefer mates with plumage similar to their own, while others have found the opposite. Pigeons fly from neighborhood to neighborhood without depending on the subway, so birds meeting on a particular street corner are probably already in agreement about important issues such as which is the best bagel shop and street vendor. What other criteria might they use in making this important decision?

A hopeful male seems to depend on his personal charisma to win the day as he walks in circles around an unattached female, bowing, cooing softly, and puffing out his handsome plumage like an avian Mr. Big. If this is enough to touch the female's heart, she may allow him to touch her feathers, and if he has just the right touch, she'll gently touch him back. Soon they are preening each other, their billing and cooing leading directly to the kind of permanent commitment Carrie Bradshaw could only dream of. The sparks of pigeon romance ignite a steady flame that endures as long as they both live.

Once paired, pigeons don't need newspaper columns, TV shows, or even the Beatles' *White Album* to inspire them to do it on

A hopeful male seems to depend on his personal charisma to win the day, puffing out his handsome plumage.

the road or wherever else they happen to be when the mood strikes. And the mood strikes often — pigeons breed in every month of the year in warm climates. In more temperate places, such as New York City, their ardor cools before winter sets in, but Valentine's Day storefronts must inspire them, because suddenly in mid-February they're back at it again.

Like many movie stars, pigeons are much more circumspect about their domestic lives than their sex lives. They build their nests in nooks and crannies of buildings, bridges, and other structures, hidden from the prying eyes of predators and paparazzi, managing rather gracefully to keep their public lives separate. Unlike many movie stars, pigeons have stable, serene private lives, but like the children of celebrities, baby pigeons really are best left out of the public eye to mature into their own selves. Soon enough they'll join their parents on the sidewalks of New York.

YOU SEND ME

Many researchers believe pigeons were domesticated more than 10,000 years ago. Ironically, it's these domestic doves, symbol of peace, that have served people in wartime. Some New York City street pigeons may be descendants of heroic birds who carried messages in the U.S. Army Signal Pigeon Corps during the two world wars.

Male or female, a pigeon's sense of home is inextricably tied to where its mate is. Once released, a pigeon will fly hundreds, sometimes thousands, of miles, winging on even through storms or bullets, just to return to its love.

RUBY-THROATED HUMMINGBIRD

Rosie the Riveter

Sixteen million Americans, mostly men, fought in World War II, and during their absence, a great many women stepped up to perform jobs from which they'd previously been excluded. Posters showing "Rosie the Riveter" helped make it socially acceptable for women to do what had traditionally been men's work even as they kept up with housekeeping and childcare.

Males spend their time at war, battling just about any living thing with the temerity to approach their defended territory.

Like prewar Americans, many bird species live with a strict division of labor by sex, but Ruby-throated Hummingbirds mirror the Rosie the Riveter era. Males spend their time at war, battling just about any living thing with the temerity to approach their defended territory. They don't just chase off other hummingbirds — they even divebomb birds as large as Bald Eagles who dare fly above their defended airspace. And as with any stereotypical World War II soldier or sailor, male hummingbirds want to spend their leave time in the company of one or more females.

Meanwhile, Rosie the Riveter stays home, finding a good spot and building her nest, lashing it to the branch with spider silk. Then all she needs to raise a family in that nest is to enlist one of those off-duty soldiers. Male hummingbirds announce their leave time by flying in a dramatic U-shaped diving loop, wings humming as they twitter as loudly as a tenth-of-an-ounce bird can. When a female shows up and perches, he switches to a "shuttle" display, flaring his brilliant ruby throat feathers, zipping side to side in a horizontal arc, and making frenzied vocalizations and wing noises.

When she tracks him with side-to-side movements of her head, makes a *mew* call, flips her tail feathers to one side, and droops her wings, he immediately alights on her back to mate. The act lasts 2 or 3 seconds, which may seem ridiculously short to us until you consider that hummingbirds pack a lot of living into every second of their lives, and he has to return to battle.

Rosie the Riveter stays home, finding a good spot and building her nest, lashing it to the branch with spider silk.

Female hummingbirds definitely connect sex with reproduction: their window of consent opens after they've prepared a nest and closes once they've produced two eggs. The females will seek out a male only on their own terms, when they are ready to start again.

The male's genetic input is not the only contribution a male hummingbird makes to his momentary mate and their young. Hummingbird eggs are so tiny that they lose heat very quickly whenever the female leaves the nest to find food, and each flower has a limited supply of nectar. The male's job, keeping all competitors away from food sources, ensures that the flowers near the nest will provide plenty of calories, minimizing the time our Rosie the Riveter spends away from her own work.

Hummingbird soldiers may never know or acknowledge their young, but they give them and their mothers their best chance for survival by waging war against anything that might dip into their nectar supplies. It's a system that works.

GOLDEN GIRLS

Female hummingbird life expectancy is longer than for males, partly because females are bigger and partly because the males' aggressive pugnaciousness puts them in peril more often. All five of the Ruby-throated Hummingbirds listed on the Bird Banding Lab's "Longevity Records" web page are females; four were recaptured, alive and well, and released again by banders when they were nine years old!

SATIN BOWERBIRD

Material Girl and Boy

Imagine a man — James Bond, Danny Ocean, or Jay Gatsby, for example — who thinks the way to attract women is by amassing wealth and displaying it as ostentatiously as possible. During his youth, he may be entirely focused on how much he has and how much more he wants to get, which does seem to attract females, but as he matures, he recognizes that a sophisticated style can help him charm even more women.

Now imagine a genuine material girl. While she's young, her only interest in any man is his wealth, but as she matures, she makes sure his personal style matches his fortune.

Most birds may not be quite as superficial as the characters we conjure up in pop culture, but bowerbirds come close. Male Satin Bowerbirds, dressed in James Bondian blacks, their violet-blue eyes as piercing as Daniel Craig's, build the entrance to their ostentatious bowers from sticks arranged in two vertical walls to create a tunnel. Beyond the tunnel, they create what they hope will be the ultimate seductive den, covered with bright and shiny objects such as berries, flowers and petals, and even metal and plastic items.

Females seem to believe that love is blue, but it takes a while for males to figure that out. As they mature, the number of blue items in their colorful arrangements increases, along with the number of females they attract.

As they mature, the number of blue items in their colorful arrangements increases, along with the number of females they attract.

The male's bower may seem as ludicrously tacky as a bachelor pad in a '60s comedy. Unlike some of the savvier leading ladies of that era, however, when a female bowerbird enters a male's tunnel of love and beholds the colorful items strewn about, especially if there's lots of blue, she falls for it.

Younger females get intimidated when a male starts his courtship dance, waving his wings and sidestepping to the accompaniment of a variety of guttural trilling sounds. These females may be wowed by shiny items but aren't so sure

how to deal with an assertive display of masculine prowess. Older females aren't so daunted.

Contrary to movies about fantasy heroes, female bowerbirds hold all the power in their relations with the opposite sex, choosing whether to enter a male's bower in the first place and then moving on after the seduction. They may return to the same male and other males as they produce eggs, always on their own terms.

A movie about bowerbirds could end when the female flies off into the sunset to raise new little bowerbirds on her own, as our James Bondian hero ends up solo in his bachelor pad. Neither one cries into its cups, "Is that all there is?" Like James Bond, both male and female bowerbirds have a rich and busy life whether in love or out of it.

LOVE NEST

In the case of bowers, the term "love nest" is strictly metaphorical. After their energetic feats of decorating, males don't help build the actual nest where eggs will be deposited, nor do they feed and protect their offspring. The material wealth of each male and the style and endurance he displays in his dance may give the female some idea about the quality of his genes, but he doesn't give anything beyond that. After all, he never promised her a rose garden.

TRUMPETER SWAN

Just the Two of Us

"You want monogamy? Marry a swan," said a character in the movie *Heartburn*. Nora Ephron was no ornithologist, but that line from her screenplay was spot on. Even when Trumpeter Swans gather in sociable migratory and winter flocks, the mated birds among them stick with their partner day in and day out. Sometimes a pair synchronize their movements as if engaging in a very private minuet.

Swan fidelity has limits: a few pairs "divorce," and widowed swans often accept a new mate by the following year. But some males who lose a mate never accept a replacement.

Unattached young or widowed birds test out the dating scene in those flocks. A few birds pair off in their second winter and may even fly off together to look for a nesting territory before their bodies are quite ready to produce young. But most swans don't rush things, waiting until their third or fourth winter to commit for a lifetime.

In early spring, the mated pairs grow restless for some private time away from the crowd, and each pair moves off to its own territory. Ideally this is an isolated shallow body of water, at least 100 yards long for their running takeoffs, with plenty of aquatic plants and muskrat or beaver dens or small islands on which to nest. They often return to the same nesting territory year after year. The same birds who weren't at all territorial in winter, in the midst of geese, ducks, cranes, and other swans, suddenly can't stand outsiders and drive away just about every trespasser. Territorial Trumpeter Swans attack trespassing coyotes and humans as well as drones and small aircraft crossing their defended air space.

When they're finally alone and spring intensifies their hormonal levels, the pair's courtship heats up, their sedate minuet breaking into the swan

> *When they're finally alone, the pair's courtship heats up, their sedate minuet breaking into the swan version of a hot tango.*

version of a hot tango. The male crosses his neck over his lady love as she extends her own neck and lowers her body in the water; this often leads to mating, the male holding his balance by grasping her neck with his bill. After copulating, they rise in the water, extend their head and neck, spread their wings, and call, ending the interlude with tail wagging and bathing. Trumpeter Swans may mate dozens of times during the week or two it takes to produce the clutch of eggs.

As incubation starts, both birds lose interest in sex, but not in each other. Steadfast devotion and constant togetherness, regardless of hormonal state, mark swan couples. The non-incubating parent moves away from the nest to feed and bathe but always stays within calling distance.

Cygnets stay very close to both parents throughout summer, fall, and winter. Come early spring, they'll be mature enough to fare for themselves, and their parents will fly off, freed from parental responsibilities just in time to start all over again.

I ONLY HAVE EYES FOR YOU

If ducks revel in raucous dancing like teenagers of the sixties, swans are more into the slow dances their hopelessly square parents performed. Two swans show an interest in each other by swimming together with an erect posture, occasionally dipping their bills in the water, sometimes romantically blowing bubbles as they lift their heads. The waterfowl around them are also swimming and sticking their bills in the water, so the subtleties of swan courtship in its early stages elude many human eyes.

WHITE-THROATED SPARROW

Romantic Comedy

*I*magine you're a screenwriter putting together a standard romantic comedy with four iconic but stereotypical lead characters: a flamboyantly beautiful, successful female CEO; a cocky, handsome male CEO; a quiet, rather mousey female kindergarten teacher; and a soft-spoken, unassuming male nurse. A good human writer could mix these characters in entirely different ways to come up with happy endings for all four. But a White-throated Sparrow could imagine just one happy ending: the female CEO must end up with the male nurse, the male CEO with the female kindergarten teacher. No other ending could possibly work out.

White-throated Sparrows come in two different plumages: half have brilliant white stripes on their head and vivid yellow lores (the area in front of the eye), and half have more muted tan stripes on their head with duller yellow lores. Both color forms are equally represented in both sexes, yet 98 percent of all mated pairs include one white-striped and one tan-striped bird.

Male and female white-striped birds all sing and are aggressively territorial. Tan-striped birds are less assertive; only males sing, and both sexes make wonderful, nurturing parents. In lab studies, nearly all males of both color forms are initially attracted to white-striped females, and nearly all females of both colors are drawn to tan-striped males.

He'd be in seventh heaven with this glamorous mate who would defend their territory so well that he could focus on his forte: nurturing the young.

With limited options, an assertive white-striped female might be forced to settle for a white-striped male. He'd be delighted — those glamorous white-striped females are genuinely alluring. But the moment she broke out in song, their relationship would be doomed. White-striped males turn into territorial bullies when they hear another White-throated Sparrow singing, even their own mate. Despite his romantic inclinations, he'd quickly drive this beautiful bird away.

She'd move on until she found a more soft-spoken tan-striped male, her preference anyway. He'd be in seventh heaven with this glamorous mate who would defend their territory so well that he could focus on his forte: nurturing the young.

If the soft-spoken tan-striped female managed to link up with her first choice, that gentle tan-striped male, they'd both be so lackadaisical about territorial defense that any neighboring white-striped male could take it over. And if a white-striped female entered the scene, the tan-striped male couldn't help but overthrow his mate for the female of his dreams.

So eventually, the bold white-striped male is left with the soft-spoken tan-striped female. Neither is the other's first choice, but their partnership, one focused on defending their family unit against territorial challenges and predators while the other nurtures the young, is just as satisfactory as that of the white-striped female and tan-striped male.

Imagine if every romantic comedy writer was required to create a male and female character who were both feisty, egotistical, and demanding, and both had to end up with a gentle, self-sacrificing, nurturing character.

Would they all live happily ever after?

IT'S COMPLICATED

The White-throated Sparrow song, a plaintive, whistled *Old Sam Peabody, Peabody, Peabody* or *O sweet Canada, Canada, Canada,* is usually sung by white-striped birds, with even odds that the singer is male or female. If a singer has tan stripes, it's definitely male. If any White-throated Sparrow is building a nest or incubating eggs, it's definitely female. Tan-striped birds of both sexes are focused on nurturing, but parents of both colors and both sexes do at least some brooding and feeding of young.

WHOOPING CRANE

Dancing with the Stars

Birds move in ways we mere humans can only dream of, yet few species use their whole bodies to dance. Male hummingbirds keep their feet tucked in during their thrilling flight displays. More down-to-earth Blue-footed Boobies keep their wings folded and unmoving in their courtship dances, flaunting their brilliant feet.

Like boobies, Whooping Cranes dance on earth rather than up in the sky, but unlike them, cranes throw their whole bodies into the performance. And unlike most displaying birds, male and female cranes dance as pairs. They sidestep, kick, run, and leap, sometimes hopping up and down as if on pogo sticks, pumping their heads up and down and then throwing the head back so the neck arches over the back, or stretching the neck so the head and bill point skyward. Meanwhile, their wings are constantly flapping or open wide for theatrical bowing.

They sidestep, kick, run, and leap, sometimes hopping up and down as if on pogo sticks.

The performance lasts about as long as many human dances, about 4 minutes. In movies, a romantic dance often leads to an even more intimate and private performance off-screen. With Whooping Cranes, once a pair is on territory, their dances end with the two mating right there on the dance floor.

Like many large birds with sizable, remote territories, Whooping Cranes mate for life. By the time cranes are 1 or 2 years old, they start "dating," meeting and spending time with other unattached cranes on their wintering grounds. As days lengthen in February and mated older pairs start courting in earnest, single birds may be inspired to attempt dancing, too. Like high schoolers, partners may back away from each other after the first dance,

THAT'S HOW STRONG MY LOVE IS

One frigid March evening at sunset, when winds were gusting to 60 miles per hour, a pair of Sandhill Cranes (closely related to Whooping Cranes) descended with a multitude of other cranes onto the Platte River in Nebraska. They flew together in perfect synchrony, wingtips often almost touching, easy to distinguish as a pair among so many others.

Battling high winds, it took them several minutes to finally alight, utterly drained. Then the male took one look at his mate, and love conquered exhaustion. He opened his wings to commence dancing, and a gust of wind plucked him up into the sky again. His mate wearily looked up and barely hesitated before opening her own wings and joining him.

but sometimes something clicks and two birds stay together a while. Whooping Cranes won't be sexually mature until they're about 4 years old. This gives them plenty of time to choose the most compatible dance and life partner.

Once a pair settles into their relationship, dancing helps cement their bond and, even more importantly, synchronizes their bodies physiologically, so both will be their most fertile at exactly the same time on their nesting territory. The urge to dance grows ever stronger the closer they get.

After nesting, cranes are grounded as they molt their flight feathers, while their young can't fly yet anyway. The pair remain inseparable through nesting and raising their one or two chicks, and they stay together with their young through the winter. Then, whether they've been together for a year or for decades, a yearning for romance hits them anew. Once again they dance with the exuberance of newlyweds and the synchronized finesse of Fred and Ginger. Their love is here to stay.

WILD TURKEY

Bully for Them

Sometimes we develop a crush on an attractive person who seems absolutely perfect right up until the first or second date, when the person reveals that what we thought was confidence and charisma was egotism and bullying.

Wild Turkey toms never pretend to be anything but bullies, but when the cockiest male gobbles and struts in spring, flaunting his swollen snood and flashy, colorful face and neck, females flock to him like teenagers chasing a pop star. This may not sound sensible, but they're not looking for a long-term relationship — just genetic material that may make their chicks as sturdy and strong as possible.

On the off-chance that another tom might have good genes, too, almost half of female turkeys hedge their bets, mating with a second or even a third male when the top tom isn't paying attention. Female turkeys lay all their eggs (up to a dozen and a half) in one basket. Those precious nest contents represent a huge investment of time, energy, and physical resources. Females naturally want to ensure that at least some of those young survive and thrive.

Turkeys establish a literal pecking order within each sex, with the "Prom King" and "Prom Queen" types dominating the social scene in each flock. Female hierarchies tend to be fairly stable, but males are forever scrabbling to move higher on the hierarchical ladder. How successful a male is at fighting isn't related to how often he fights. Some males never quit sparring with other males even as they lose most of their matches, while some excellent fighters stay in shape by avoiding fights unless pressed.

When a flock of males meets another during the breeding season, all the members join together as a team to fight the other flock. Like human football teams, these flocks are ranked, and females prefer to mate with the top tom on a winning team.

Males are forever scrabbling to move higher on the hierarchical ladder.

All that hormone-fueled drama dissipates by autumn. As the brilliant bare skin on males grows more subdued and their snoods are no longer swollen, they settle into fairly large flocks for the winter. Like most high school football teams, male flocks never include females; the boys show off to nearby females during the breeding season, but except during the actual mating game, males stick to their own kind.

Summer female flocks include male as well as female poults, but by summer's end and autumn, as the young males outgrow their mothers, most of them gravitate to boys' clubs. Fortunately, this happens right when the older males are taking a winter recess from all the drama and aggressiveness of high school social life.

Soon enough, spring comes. Once again, hormones surge, there's a flurry of socializing, and even the calmest females will find themselves chasing one cocky heartthrob. The main difference between Wild Turkeys and high schoolers is that, one day, most high schoolers grow up.

TURKEY TIME

Hunting season for most animals falls in autumn, after the breeding season is over. This provides a large harvest while minimizing impact on reproduction, to ensure that the hunt is sustainable. But many states provide a spring season on Wild Turkeys, even as the turkey population surges. In spring, hunters use turkey calls to target male turkeys ("gobblers"). Most of these males wouldn't be mating with the females anyway, and so reducing their numbers won't affect that season's reproduction at all.

WILSON'S PHALAROPE

Wearing the Pants

In many territorial bird species, it's the male who claims and defends the territory. And males of many species, such as hawks, are the family "breadwinners," doing all the hunting for food as the females incubate eggs and brood the babies, at least until the young are big enough to need provisioning by both parents. Many species share responsibilities rather evenly after the eggs hatch, and males of some species, such as loons and Rose-breasted Grosbeaks, even share incubating duties.

But birds of a few species, such as a dainty shorebird called Wilson's Phalarope, turn our expectations of sex roles entirely on their head. Females are significantly larger and more brightly colorful than males. And it's the females who aggressively defend the territory and compete for mates, even breaking out into fights with other females over the males.

Once a female Wilson's Phalarope attracts a male, she doesn't let him out of her sight. It's very hard to find a paired phalarope more than 3 feet from its mate during their brief but intense honeymoon stage.

The female is usually the one to initiate sex, the male more than happy to oblige. She makes the first small scrape on the ground where she wants the nest to be, and he doesn't second-guess her even though he's the one who will fuss with it, tidying the area and arranging surrounding plants to hide the nest. Within a few days she'll lay an egg. A day or two later, she'll lay a second egg, and then a third, as the pair continues to mate frequently.

When the third egg is laid, the male is the one who grows broody and starts incubating. The female, physiologically incapable of incubating or even developing a brood patch, doesn't seem to have any concept of parental duties. It's possible she doesn't even know there's a chick in each one of those eggs. But she stays near, mating with her partner when he's off the nest and chasing off any females who approach, until she lays the fourth and final egg. At that point, the honeymoon is over.

> *When the third egg is laid, the male is the one who grows broody and starts incubating.*

Some females hightail it out of there immediately. Some stick around for at least a day or two, defending the vulnerable incubating male. A lingering farewell holds no promise of romantic attraction, however, and every female moves on before her eggs hatch, 3 or so weeks after incubation started. The Mr. Moms take single parenthood in stride. It's the only system they've ever known.

When weather and food are optimal, females move on once or twice to new territories to mate with new males. When nesting is over for the season, phalaropes gather in large, convivial flocks with no sexual drama at all. Hormones won't break up these sociable flocks until spring.

WHIRL POWER

Phalaropes feed using a charming technique: they spin like little tops at the water's surface, each one creating a whirlpool that draws insects up to the surface where the dainty birds can reach them. The technique is so effective that in the salty, nutrient-rich lakes where they stop to molt during migration, some phalaropes can even double their weight. That fat fuels their journey to wintering grounds in South America.

Epilogue

One winter, a chickadee with a badly overgrown bill and deformed foot came to my hand many times a day for mealworms. I was as thrilled to see him as he was to see me crank open the window.

The overgrown part of his bill broke off at winter's end, too late for him to attract a mate that year. But the following year he found a mate, and they nested near my house. I felt deeply invested in his success.

The more we know birds, the more we care about them, and that's true not only for individuals we know personally. Watching a woodcock dancing in the sunset sky, I feel a surge of hope that females are watching and listening and find him as wonderful as I do. When a male crow gently nuzzles his mate's neck in a secluded spot in my big spruce; or a pair of Piping Plovers searches for food on an open beach, keeping track of the other's every move; or a pair of swans swims together in perfect synchrony, my heart swells with love and concern. *To love* is an active verb. Some things you can do to help:

» Be a conservation-conscious consumer. In particular, avoid plastics of all kinds, which many oceanic birds mistake for food.

» Identify and keep track of the birds in your own neighborhood. Reporting them to eBird.org will give conservation biologists important information over time.

» Grow an assortment of locally native trees, shrubs, and other plants to provide food and cover for a variety of birds. Root out invasive plants. Eliminate or minimize the use of lawn and garden insecticides.

» Learn about the pros and cons of bird feeding, and how and when to safely offer birdseed, peanut butter and nuts, suet, fruits and jellies, and calcium and other minerals. The Cornell Lab of Ornithology's FeederWatch.org is a great place to get started.

» Offer appropriate nesting materials. Provide nest boxes and platforms, and monitor them responsibly. Cornell's NestWatch.org will help.

» Birds may cause inconveniences. Try to respond responsibly and proactively.

» Support your favorite birding spots. Be responsible when visiting public parks and gardens, and practice low-impact hiking. Foster a culture of conservation in your own neighborhood.

» Report banded birds to the Bird Banding Laboratory (www.usgs.gov/centers/pwrc/science/bird-banding-laboratory).

» Volunteer at conservation organizations, and work to make strong environmental protections part of your political party's agenda.

» Binoculars: don't leave home without 'em. The more we observe birds, the more we know them; and the more we know them, the more we care about them.

» You can learn more at lauraerickson.com/ways-to-help.